...ENTS

Pedigree

Published by Pedigree Books Limited
Beech Hill House, Walnut Gardens, Exeter, Devon EX4 4DH
email: books@pedigreegroup.co.uk Published 2009

PROFILE:

JOHN CENA®

HEIGHT
6-foot-1
WEIGHT
240 pounds
FROM
West Newbury, MA
SIGNATURE MOVE
Attitude Adjustment, STF
CAREER HIGHLIGHTS
WWE Champion
World Heavyweight Champion
United States Champion
World Tag Team Champion
2008 Royal Rumble Winner

RAW

SINCE making his debut in 2002, John Cena has gone on to become one of the most popular and successful Superstars of his generation. At *WrestleMania XX* he captured his first Championship, the United States Championship, by defeating Big Show in a match that many considered an upset. By the following year, at *WrestleMania 21*, Cena had cemented his place as a main event Superstar. He defeated John 'Bradshaw' Layfield for the WWE Championship in a hard fought match. Throughout 2006, Cena battled Edge for the championship, capturing the gold twice more at the *Royal Rumble* and at *Unforgiven*. In January, 2007, Cena teamed with Shawn Michaels to capture his first Tag Team Championship. The pair failed to coexist and lost the Championships just a few weeks later. In 2008, the unlikely paring of Cena and Batista defeated Cody Rhodes and Ted DiBiase to earn Cena his second Tag Team Championship.
In August of 2008, John Cena suffered a serious neck injury after taking two Batista Bombs at *SummerSlam*, he would be out of action for three months. On his return, Cena shocked the world by defeating World Heavyweight Champion, Chris Jericho for the title in his first match back.

PROFILE:

CM PUNK®

HEIGHT
6-foot-1
WEIGHT
222 pounds
FROM
Chicago, Il
SIGNATURE MOVE
G.T.S. (Go To Sleep)
Anaconda Vise
CAREER HIGHLIGHTS
World Heavyweight Champion
ECW Champion
Intercontinental Champion
World Tag Team Champion

RAW®

SINCE his debut in 2006, CM Punk's rise to the top has been meteoric. Punk made his WWE debut in *ECW*, defeating *ECW* original, Stevie Richards. It would not be long until the other *ECW* Superstars would stand up and take notice of the young upstart. With his straight edged lifestyle, tattoos and incredible repertoire of moves, it was obvious that Punk would become a force to be reckoned with. At *Survivor Series 2006*, Punk teamed with The Hardys and DX to form a team the likes of which had never been seen before. Punk impressed his veteran partners that night, so much so that Triple H called him 'The future of WWE'! By the summer of 2007, Punk had proven himself to be a main event contender and on September 4th, he defeated John Morrison for the *ECW* Championship. At *WrestleMania XXIV*, Punk won the Money in the Bank Ladder Match, earning him a shot at then Champion, Edge for the World Heavyweight Championship. On June 30th, 2008, Punk shocked the world by cashing in his Money in the Bank contract and defeating Edge for the gold!

WORD SEARCH

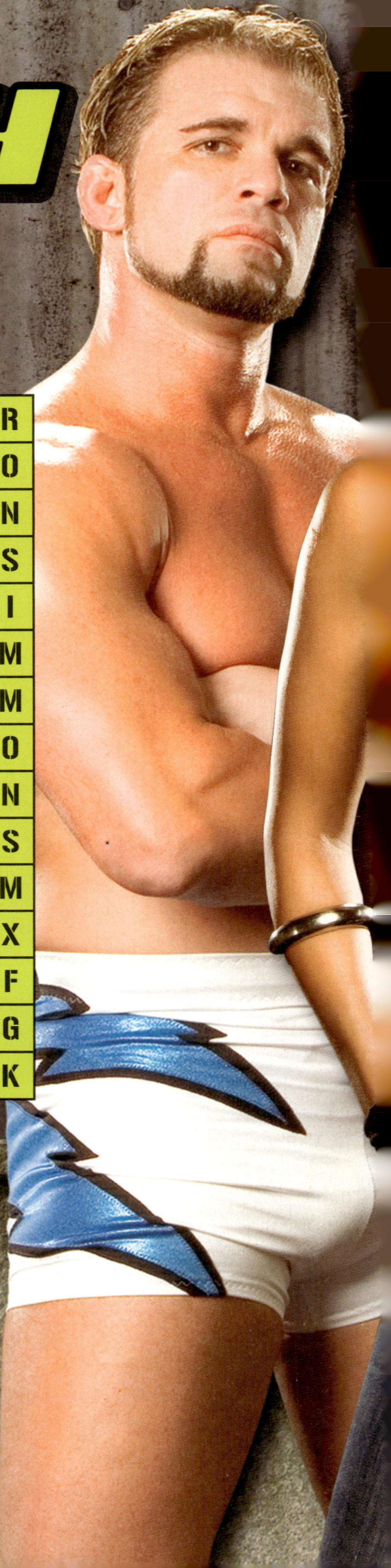

CAN YOU FIND ALL 10 OF THE *RAW* SUPERSTARS HIDDEN IN THIS WORD SEARCH PUZZLE?

Q	R	G	E	A	W	R	S	D	O	U	H	L	L	R
V	N	C	N	V	W	E	Z	F	C	M	I	C	E	O
J	R	G	A	J	B	L	T	R	M	Y	V	M	W	N
H	H	U	K	E	X	G	C	R	Y	S	U	S	O	S
Q	S	P	D	V	B	G	H	W	O	Q	A	L	P	I
R	L	A	V	M	H	I	Z	J	I	A	Y	G	O	M
P	H	M	X	V	G	Z	O	M	H	I	M	S	Z	M
S	A	N	M	I	C	H	A	E	L	C	O	L	E	O
I	D	L	T	Z	N	P	I	O	R	X	S	E	T	N
H	B	V	Y	C	X	L	E	C	I	D	N	A	C	S
O	F	W	E	A	R	O	T	F	Q	N	E	B	C	M
R	U	N	N	A	L	D	P	F	W	O	Y	B	T	X
E	A	B	H	F	H	T	B	A	P	B	R	T	A	F
C	A	C	V	J	L	V	Z	F	D	G	L	V	Q	G
J	O	I	X	R	J	V	Q	Y	M	A	N	U	K	K

- CANDICE
- CHARLIE HAAS
- DOLPH ZIGGLER
- JOHN CENA
- KANE
- LAYLA
- MANU
- MICHAEL COLE
- RON SIMMONS
- SHAD

CROSSWORD

CAN YOU USE ALL YOUR KNOWLEDGE OF THE *RAW* SUPERSTARS TO SOLVE THE CLUES AND REVEAL THE ANSWERS?

ACROSS

3. Undertaker's half brother
5. The colour of the *Raw* ring ropes
8. Blackpool's Bad Boy!
9. Son of the Superfly!
10. Perhaps the highest vertical leap in WWE

DOWN

1. A former Cruiserweight Champion
2. *Raw's* ring announcer
4. The hottest ring entrance ever!
6. He trained The Brian Kendrick
7. Nice beard dude!

PROFILE:
KOFI KINGSTON™

HEIGHT
6-foot-1
WEIGHT
200 pounds
FROM
Jamaica
SIGNATURE MOVE
Cool Running's
CAREER HIGHLIGHTS
Intercontinental Champion
World Tag Team Champion

RAW®

HAILING from the tropical climate of the Caribbean, Jamaican Superstar Kofi Kingston brings unique in-ring abilities, style and lingo to *Raw*.

For weeks, WWE fans were offered a glimpse into Kingston's island paradise where the vibrant Superstar took troublesome matters into his own capable hands. Mixing it up with his lightning quick arsenal while maintaining his bright, amiable smile, Kofi undoubtedly made *ECW* his own private Island of the Extreme.

Kofi first engaged in a series of matches against Shelton Benjamin. Although he had done incredibly well in them, Benjamin is responsible for giving Kingston his first loss in WWE. Rather than slowing him down, this has only inspired Kofi to work harder and do even better in the future.

The day after defeating *ECW's* Gold Standard in an Extreme Rules Match, Kofi Kingston was drafted to *Raw* in the Supplemental Draft on 25 June. Since then, the Jamaican Superstar has made an impact on Monday nights, first winning the Intercontinental Championship from Chris Jericho, then becoming World Tag Team Champion with CM Punk.

PROFILE:

CANDICE®

HEIGHT
5-foot-7
FROM
Milwaukee, WI
SIGNATURE MOVE
Candy Wrapper
CAREER HIGHLIGHTS
Women's Champion

RAW®

IF there's one thing Candice Michelle is determined to prove, it's that she's not just another pretty face. And she seemed to prove it by winning the WWE Women's Championship and holding on to it for almost three months. Since becoming a WWE Diva, Candice has maintained her beautiful image while continuing to improve her in-ring skills. Working with legendary Four Horsemen enforcer Arn Anderson, her development is evident every time she steps into the ring. From physical battles to the vaunted Lingerie Pillow Fight, Candice is not afraid to mix it up in any way. Her training and her heart have paid off with the Women's Championship. Candice embodies the spirit of a true WWE Diva - being a woman who can kick butt and look good doing it. With her particularly striking combination of good looks, in-ring ability and bubbly personality, this self-professed 'Cheese Head' from Wisconsin could someday be considered one of the greatest WWE Divas ever.

RAW

QUIZ

LETS FIND OUT JUST HOW MUCH YOU KNOW ABOUT YOUR FAVOURITE SUPERSTARS OF *RAW!*

Q1

WHICH TAG TEAM CO-PRESENTED AN AWARD WITH CANDICE AT THE 2008 SLAMMY AWARD SHOW?

A: Cryme Tyme ☐
B: Jesse and Festus ☐
C: Carlito and Primo Colon ☐

Q2

WHO IS THIS *RAW* SUPERSTAR?

A: Hardcore Holly ☐
B: Dolph Ziggler ☐
C: Cody Rhodes ☐

Q3

WHAT IS RON SIMMONS' CATCHPHRASE?

A: Damn! ☐
B: Ooops! ☐
C: La De Da! ☐

Q4

GOLDUST IS THE SON OF WHICH WWE LEGEND?

A: Jake 'The Snake' Roberts ☐
B: Bobby 'The Brain' Heenan ☐
C: Dusty Rhodes ☐

Q5

IN WHAT YEAR WAS REY MYSTERIO FIRST DRAFTED TO *RAW*?

A: 2006 ☐
B: 2007 ☐
C: 2008 ☐

Q6

WHICH FORMER *RAW* GENERAL MANAGER WAS FIRED AND DUMPED IN THE BACK OF A RUBBISH TRUCK BY MR MCMAHON?

A: Mike Adamle ☐
B: Eric Bischoff ☐
C: Stephanie McMahon ☐

Q7

WHO IS THIS *RAW* SUPERSTAR?

A: Kelly Kelly ☐
B: Jillian ☐
C: Lilian Garcia ☐

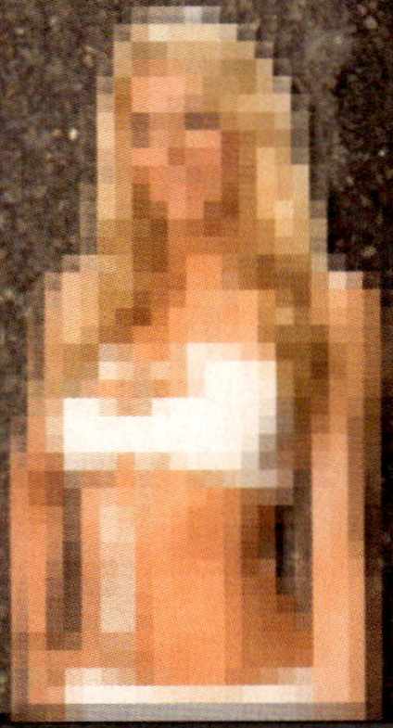

Q8

WHO WON THE *2008 KING OF THE RING* TOURNAMENT?

A: CM Punk ☐
B: Mr Kennedy ☐
C: William Regal ☐

Q9

WHO DID MIKE KNOX ASSAULT ON HIS SECOND NIGHT AS A *RAW* SUPERSTAR?

A: Rey Mysterio ☐
B: Evan Bourne ☐
C: John Cena ☐

Q10

CAN YOU TELL WHICH *RAW* DIVA THIS IS FROM JUST HER EYES?

A: Melina ☐
B: Candice ☐
C: Mickie James ☐

(ANSWERS: 1.A, 2.B, 3.A, 4.C, 5.C, 6.B, 7.A, 8.C, 9.B, 10.A)

WHO

Q1

'I DON'T DRINK AND I DON'T SMOKE, I DON'T DO DRUGS. MY ADDICTION IS WRESTLING. WITH NO TOXINS AND NO DISTRACTIONS, I'VE BEEN ABLE TO MAKE AN IMPACT WITH WORLD WRESTLING ENTERTAINMENT. BUT I STILL WANT TO GO FARTHER.'

Q2

'THESE ARE NOT JUST CATCHY SLOGANS. I NEVER GIVE UP AND I NEVER SURRENDER. HUSTLE. LOYALTY. RESPECT. THERE'S ALWAYS GOING TO BE SOMEONE BIGGER, OR FASTER, OR MEANER. BUT I MAKE SURE THERE'S NO ONE MORE DETERMINED THAN I AM.'

Q3

'I AM HERE TO ENTERTAIN THE PEOPLE, TO SAVE THEM FROM THEIR BOREDOM, THEIR AGONY. THE ADULATION OF THE MILLIONS OF JERICHAHOLICS IS ALL THE THANKS I NEED. WELL, MAYBE A CHAMPIONSHIP REIGN OR TWO THROWN IN FOR GOOD MEASURE, HUH?'

MELINA

JOHN CENA

REY MYSTERIO

SAID DAT?

SOMETIMES IN THE WWE UNIVERSE, WHAT IS SAID OUTSIDE THE RING CAN BE JUST AS HARD HITTING AS THE ACTION INSIDE THE RING! CAN YOU MATCH EACH OF THESE QUOTES TO THE SUPERSTAR THAT SAID THEM?

Q4

'WHETHER YOU LOVE ME OR HATE ME, YOU CAN'T HELP BUT WATCH ME'

Q5

'WWE CAN BE A PRETTY HARSH LANDSCAPE WHEN YOU GO IT ALONE AND A FEW BOMBS ALWAYS HELP TO LEVEL THE TERRAIN'

Q6

'JBL, I DON'T RESPECT YOU EITHER. I ACTUALLY FIGHT. YOU GET MARK HENRY AND THE GREAT KHALI TO DO YOUR DIRTY WORK. WHAT'S THE MATTER, DON'T YOU HAVE THE COJONES TO FACE ME YOURSELF?'

CM PUNK ☐ BATISTA ☐ CHRIS JERICHO ☐

(ANSWERS: 1. CM PUNK, 2. JOHN CENA, 3. CHRIS JERICHO, 4. MELINA, 5. BATISTA, 6. REY MYSTERIO)

PROFILE:

WILLIAM REGAL®

HEIGHT
6-foot-2

WEIGHT
240 pounds

FROM
Blackpool, England

SIGNATURE MOVE
Regal Stretch, Power of the Punch

CAREER HIGHLIGHTS
Intercontinental Champion
World Tag Team Champion
European Champion
Hardcore Champion
WCW Television Champion
WWE Commissioner
Alliance Commissioner
Raw General Manager
2008 WWE *King of the Ring*

RAW®

NORMALLY, William Regal is one of WWE's most smug and haughty Superstars. A distinguished Englishman, Regal finds most others crass and downright unworthy of his time. While presenting himself as a dignified man away from the ring, Regal is a sadistic mat wrestler inside it, taking great pleasure in torturing his adversaries with stiff strikes and brutal submission holds.

The Englishman also used his class and wit to determine the week-to-week function of the entire Monday night roster as the General Manager of *Raw*, keeping in line fans and competitors alike. Arguably his crowning achievement, however, was becoming literally regal by winning the 2008 WWE *King of the Ring* Tournament. Then in late 2008, in front of all his countrymen in Manchester, England, William Regal became the new Intercontinental Champion by defeating Santino Marella in quick and decisive fashion.

PROFILE:

CODY RHODES®

HEIGHT
6-foot-1
WEIGHT
219 pounds
FROM
Charlotte, NC
SIGNATURE MOVE
Rolling Cutter
CAREER HIGHLIGHTS
World Tag Team Championship

RAW®

AS the son of WWE Hall of Famer the 'American Dream' Dusty Rhodes, Cody Rhodes grew up admiring his father and watching him capture the imagination of wrestling fans worldwide. Now Cody is ready to carry on his father's legacy while carving out one of his own in WWE. Cody's road to success started when he teamed with Hardcore Holly, as the two captured the World Tag Team Championship in 2007. That partnership would not last however as at *Night of Champions*, Cody turned his back on his mentor and joined forces with another second generation Superstar, Ted DiBiase. The pair double teamed Holly and captured the gold that night. Since then, Rhodes and DiBiase have been a force to be reckoned with in the tag team division, even defeating the formidable team of Batista and John Cena to capture the Championship for a second time. Most recently, this devious duo has fallen under the influence of the Legend Killer, Randy Orton and dubbed themselves The Legacy. United in their assault on the *Raw* roster, there is no telling how much chaos these multi-generational Superstars will cause.

GUESS THE SUPERSTAR

Q1

I MADE MY WWE DEBUT IN 1995. I AM A FORMER INTERCONTINENTAL CHAMPION AND WORLD TAG TEAM CHAMPION. WHEN I FIRST ENTERED WWE, MY WIFE AND MANAGER CAME WITH ME. HER NAME WAS MARLENA. MY SIGNATURE MOVE IS CALLED THE CURTAIN CALL.

Q2

I AM A THIRD GENERATION SUPERSTAR. I HAVE HELD THE WWE CHAMPIONSHIP AND WORLD HEAVYWEIGHT CHAMPIONSHIP ALONG WITH THE INTERCONTINENTAL CHAMPIONSHIP AND THE WORLD TAG TEAM CHAMPIONSHIP WITH EDGE.

Q3

I STARTED MY WWE CAREER IN 1995 AS PART OF A TAG TEAM NAMED THE ACOLYTES. ORIGINALLY PART OF UNDERTAKER'S MINISTRY OF DARKNESS. I HAVE ALSO HAD MAJOR SUCCESS IN THE BUSINESS WORLD

REY MYSTERIO ☐

RANDY ORTON ☐

JBL ☐

CAN YOU MATCH EACH OF THESE DESCRIPTIONS TO THE *RAW* SUPERSTARS BELOW?

Q4

I STAND 6-FOOT TALL AND WEIGH 221 POUNDS. I USED TO WRESTLE AT THE AMATEUR LEVEL AT KENT STATE UNIVERSITY WHERE I WON MORE MATCHES THAN ANYONE ELSE ON THE TEAM. I MADE MY WWE DEBUT IN 2009 ON *RAW* AFTER WEEKS OF INTRODUCING MYSELF TO THE FANS.

Q5

I AM A FORMER MEMBER OF EVOLUTION. I STARTED MY CAREER ON *SMACKDOWN* TEAMING WITH THE REVEREND D-VON. I WON THE *ROYAL RUMBLE* IN 2005 AND WENT ON TO DEFEAT TRIPLE H FOR MY FIRST WORLD HEAVYWEIGHT CHAMPIONSHIP AT *WRESTLEMANIA 21*. I WAS DRAFTED BACK TO *RAW* IN 2008.

Q6

I WEIGH JUST 175 POUNDS. I EXPLODED ONTO THE U.S. WRESTLING SCENE IN THE EARLY 90'S IN *ECW*. I SOON FOUND MYSELF IN WCW WHERE I CAPTURED THE CRUISERWEIGHT CHAMPIONSHIP ON SEVERAL OCCASIONS. MY BATTLES WITH THE LATE EDDIE GUERRERO ARE SOME OF THE BEST MATCHES I HAVE EVER HAD.

DOLPH ZIGGLER ☐ BATISTA ☐ GOLDUST ☐

(ANSWERS: 1. GOLDUST, 2. RANDY ORTON, 3. JBL, 4. DOLPH ZIGGLER, 5. BATISTA, 6. REY MYSTERIO)

PROFILE:

MIKE KNOX®

HEIGHT
6-foot-6
WEIGHT
293 pounds
FROM
Phoenix, AZ
SIGNATURE MOVE
Spinning Reverse STO

MIKE KNOX is one of WWE's most vicious Superstars and his mean streak has left none safe - not even his former girlfriend, Kelly Kelly. Knox grew angry with the blond bombshell when she publicly proclaimed her admiration for *ECW* Superstar CM Punk. Knox stunned fans when he attacked Kelly with a Spinning Reverse STO, violently ending their relationship.

Knox is just as dangerous inside the ring as well. Since his first day in *ECW*, Knox has been relentless and collected a number of victories over the Land of the Extreme's toughest competitors. His move to *Monday Night Raw* can only mean physical misery ahead for the Raw roster. Just ask Rey Mysterio, who has been on the receiving side of many a brutal attack from the vicious Knox since his *Raw* debut.

PROFILE: JBL™

HEIGHT
6-foot-6
WEIGHT
290 pounds
FROM
New York City
SIGNATURE MOVE
Clothesline From Hell
CAREER HIGHLIGHTS
WWE Champion
World Tag Team Champion
United States Champion
Hardcore Champion
European Champion

RAW®

JOHN BRADSHAW LAYFIELD started his WWE career in 1995 as part of a tag team named The Acolytes. Originally part of Undertaker's Ministry of Darkness, JBL and Farooq, (Ron Simmons) would go on to become one of the most devastating Tag Team combinations of their era. The APA, as they became known, captured the World Tag Team Championship on three occasions and were involved in some of the greatest tag team matches in the history of WWE.

In 2004, The APA spilt, leaving JBL as a singles competitor on *SmackDown*. Getting physical in the ring has netted JBL a career wealth of championships, while his 'fiscal' approach to the stock market has made him a very bankable resource in shareholders' eyes. Perhaps the one drawback from his economic success is that it affords him the luxury of saying whatever's on his mind-mainly because he can put his money where his mouth is. And since his return to in-ring competition in early 2008, JBL has also put his boot where his opponents' mouths are.

JBL is not only an extremely talented WWE Superstar, he has also had major success in the business world. He is a senior vice-president at a major investment bank. Analysts respect his appearances on *Fox News Channel*, *CNN*, *CNNfn*, *MSNBC*, *CNBC*, and *C-SPAN* as a financial advisor, not a "wrestling god." He didn't need a degree in Finance to line people's pockets with cash, or provide common-sense management tips in his bestselling book *Have More Money Now*. And "The John Bradshaw Layfield Show," a weekly radio program, in which he champions his views on politics, sports, and entertainment, is now syndicated in more than 150 radio stations across America.

LEGENDS

QUIZ

HOW MUCH DO YOU KNOW ABOUT THE MEN AND WOMEN WHO PIONEERED SPORTS ENTERTAINMENT? FIND OUT RIGHT HERE!

Q1

WHICH WWE LEGEND WAS KNOWN AS 'THE AMERICAN DREAM'?

A: Dusty Rhodes ☐
B: Vader ☐
C: Bam Bam Bigelow ☐

Q2

WHO IS THIS WWE LEGEND?

A: The Iron Sheik ☐
B: British Bulldog ☐
C: Ted DiBiase ☐

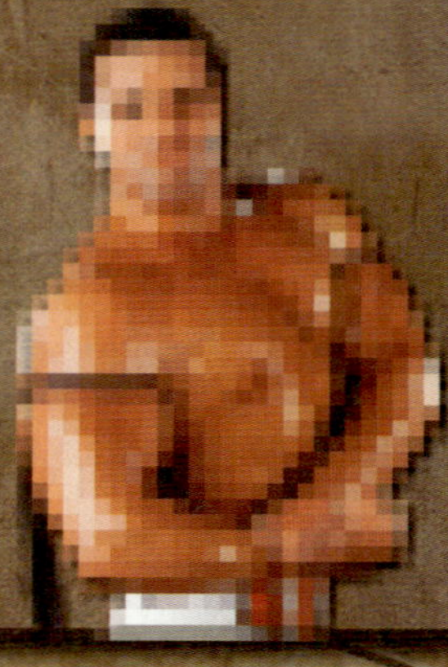

Q3

WHICH WWE LEGEND USED TO CALL THE FANS 'PENCIL-NECKED GEEKS'?

- **A:** Bobby 'The Brain' Heenan ☐
- **B:** Jake 'The Snake' Roberts ☐
- **C:** 'Classie' Freddie Blassie ☐

Q4

WHO WAS THE FIRST MAN TO HOLD THE INTERCONTINENTAL CHAMPIONSHIP?

- **A:** Don Muraco ☐
- **B:** Pat Patterson ☐
- **C:** Greg Valentine ☐

Q5

WHO IS THIS FORMER WWE CHAMPION?

- **A:** Sgt. Slaughter ☐
- **B:** Bob Backlund ☐
- **C:** The Iron Sheik ☐

Q6

FOR HOW MANY MONTHS DID THE HONKY TONK MAN HOLD THE INTERCONTINENTAL CHAMPIONSHIP?

- **A:** 11 ☐
- **B:** 12 ☐
- **C:** 14 ☐

Q7

WHO WAS THE FIRST MAN TO HOLD THE WWE CHAMPIONSHIP?

- **A:** Buddy Rogers ☐
- **B:** Bob Backlund ☐
- **C:** Hulk Hogan ☐

Q8

WHO IS THIS FORMER WWE SUPERSTAR?

- **A:** Vader ☐
- **B:** Damien Demento ☐
- **C:** Paul Bearer ☐

Q9

IN WHAT YEAR DID ANDRE THE GIANT FIRST CAPTURE THE WWE CHAMPIONSHIP?

- **A:** 1986 ☐
- **B:** 1988 ☐
- **C:** 1990 ☐

Q10

WHO WAS THE FIRST EVER WWE WOMEN'S CHAMPION IN 1956?

- **A:** Mae Young ☐
- **B:** Fabulous Moolah ☐
- **C:** Sherri Martel ☐

(ANSWERS. 1.A, 2.B, 3.C, 4.B, 5.A, 6.C, 7.A, 8.A, 9.B, 10.B)

PROFILE:

BOBBY HEENAN™

FROM

Beverly Hills, CA

MANY of the smartest minds in sports entertainment consider Bobby Heenan to be the greatest manager to have ever set foot in the ring. And who could argue with them? Bobby Heenan excelled in every aspect of his role. He could talk a blue streak on the mic like no one before or since, making himself a valuable mouthpiece for anyone he represented. His comedic talents were priceless. And when it came time to pay the piper for all his evil deeds, no one could take a beating like 'The Brain.'

He managed some of the greatest Superstars WWE has ever seen, men like Mr Perfect, the Blackjacks, Big John Studd, King Kong Bundy, 'Ravishing' Rick Rude, Arn Anderson & Tully Blanchard and Harley Race. Perhaps his greatest managerial success came with a true icon of the business, Andre the Giant. Heenan actually accompanied Andre to the ring at *WrestleMania III* in front of 93,173 fans at the Pontiac Silverdome in 1987.

As good a manager as he was, Heenan also made a name for himself behind the announcer's desk. His partnership with the late, great Gorilla Monsoon is the stuff of legend. The two are generally regarded as the Abbott and Costello of sports entertainment due to their incredibly funny banter. Heenan is also one of the only commentators to have sat in the booth for both *Raw* and *Monday Nitro*.

Bobby 'The Brain' Heenan now resides in Florida with his wife and claims to have retired from sports entertainment. Still, you never know when 'The Weasel' will pop up again!

PROFILE:

BRET HART™

FROM
Calgary, Alberta

SIGNATURE MOVE
Sharpshooter

CAREER HIGHLIGHTS
WWE Champion
Intercontinental Champion
World Tag Team Champion
King of the Ring
1994 *Royal Rumble* co-winner
WCW Champion
WCW United States Champion
WCW Tag Team Champion

KNOWN as the 'Excellence of Execution,' Bret Hart was one of the finest technical wrestlers ever. This submission specialist was known for systematically breaking down his opponents until he was ready to lock in the Sharpshooter, from which few escaped. Hart was also an innovator in the ring, executing strategies and applying holds (such as the ring-post figure-four leglock) that defied the expectations of opponents and fans alike. Hart also had an uncanny instinct for creating pinning predicaments out of opponents' holds when things looked their most bleak.

The 'Hit Man' was trained with his brothers and other Calgary hopefuls in the infamous Stu Hart Dungeon. It was there that his father stressed technique over flair, and it was there that Bret mastered an arsenal of submission manoeuvres the hardest way possible – by having them applied to him.

After achieving great success with WWE for over a decade, Hart left for WCW in 1997, where he added to his championship accolades until retiring from active competition in 2002.

Despite the premature end of his wrestling career, Hart remains one of the biggest names in the history of sports-entertainment. He was inducted into the WWE Hall Of Fame in 2006 by one of his greatest opponents, Stone Cold Steve Austin, and remains one of the most popular Superstars ever to step in the ring.

ECW

CROSSWORD

HOW EXTREME ARE YOU? DO YOU KNOW ENOUGH ABOUT THE *ECW* SUPERSTARS TO SOLVE THESE CLUES AND REVEAL THE ANSWERS? LET'S SEE SHALL WE?

ACROSS

2. The Suplex Machine!
6. His shooting star press is simply amazing!
7. This guy loves to inflict pain!
8. He lies, he cheats, and he steals!
9. Some guys think they are tough eating nails for breakfast. I eat worms!

DOWN

1. He defeated Matt Hardy for the *ECW* Championship in January 2009
2. The innovator of violence
3. He will not die!
4. The strongest man in *ECW* history!
5. *ECW* commentator

WORD SEARCH

CAN YOU FIND ALL TEN OF THE *ECW* SUPERSTARS HIDING IN THIS WORD SEARCH? FIND THEM QUICK, BEFORE THEY SLAM YOU THROUGH A TABLE!

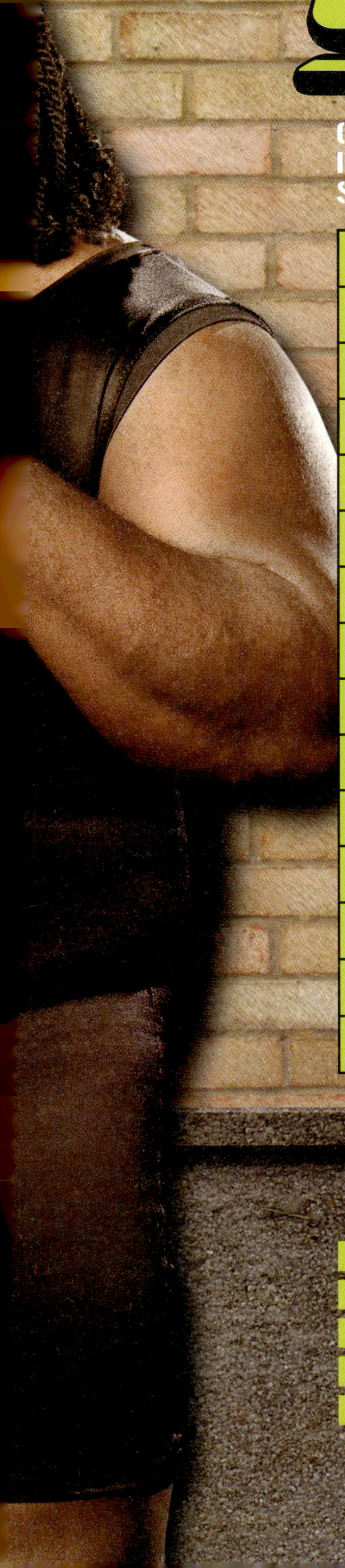

R	A	Y	G	X	Y	O	O	U	A	W	T	Y	B	X
I	I	T	D	A	F	O	J	L	V	E	O	N	N	E
A	P	C	L	R	C	X	I	V	L	I	N	A	W	D
V	P	N	K	M	A	C	F	G	Y	N	Y	F	F	S
M	I	Y	D	Y	I	H	G	V	A	Y	A	F	M	Y
F	M	P	O	A	O	O	T	N	K	C	T	I	P	I
P	U	V	F	U	W	R	Y	T	Y	E	L	T	O	K
J	U	O	N	S	M	L	T	Z	A	W	A	R	K	Q
M	X	K	N	T	H	E	M	I	Z	M	S	X	L	P
Z	R	R	Q	R	C	R	B	O	Z	E	E	G	X	M
M	O	L	E	I	R	B	A	G	J	D	Z	T	X	P
H	Y	L	M	D	P	T	Y	V	O	H	N	U	V	D
D	U	S	T	Y	R	H	O	D	E	S	A	L	T	U
C	N	U	D	Y	H	S	C	D	Z	F	A	M	V	K
T	Q	S	Y	Q	M	T	F	B	C	Q	P	X	R	M

- ALICIA FOX
- DJ GABRIEL
- FINLAY
- DUSTY RHODES
- HORNSWOGGLE
- MATT HARDY
- RICKY ORTIZ
- THE MIZ
- TIFFANY
- TONY ATLAS

PROFILE:

EVAN BOURNE™

HEIGHT
5-foot-9
WEIGHT
183 pounds
FROM
St. Louis, MO
SIGNATURE MOVE
Shooting Star Press
WWE DEBUT
June 2008

ECW®

BOURNE started his in-ring training at 17 years old. Before long, he had become the first person under the age of 18 to be licensed to wrestle in the state of Missouri. It was during his very first match, while connecting with a difficult moonsault, that a familiar feeling washed over him and left no doubt in his mind that he was doing what he was meant to do. Bourne's quest to join WWE eventually took him all over the United States, Europe and Japan. During this time, he became very accomplished, winning several honours including St. Louis' Wrestler of the Year in 2006 and Move of the Year in 2007 for his Shooting Star Press.

In 2008, Bourne blasted onto the *ECW* scene, giving the WWE Universe an exciting combination of Mexican, Japanese, and American training styles that has made him both a dangerous high-flyer and a sound ground technician.

Overall, Bourne is very excited about being a part of the Land of Extreme and feels it will give him a perfect opportunity to give WWE fans a creative, unique style that they have never seen before. In the months to come, Bourne has set his sights on proving himself and earning the respect of one and all.

PROFILE:

JOHN MORRISON®

WEIGHT
219 pounds
FROM
Los Angeles, CA
SIGNATURE MOVE
Snapshot, Moonlight Drive
CAREER HIGHLIGHTS
ECW Champion
Intercontinental Champion
WWE Tag Team Champion
World Tag Team Champion

ECW®

JOHN MORRISON endured a personal evolution of sorts after capturing the vacated *ECW* Championship at Vengeance: Night of Champions 2007. The Tuesday Night Delight, formerly known as Johnny Nitro, officially renamed himself John Morrison, his given birth name, on the historic 17 July 2007, edition of *ECW*. Morrison had reached the peak of his fame with the *ECW* Championship and he believed he could 'be himself' from that point forward.

Shortly thereafter, Morrison found unexpected success alongside another brazen, rising star in the Land of Extreme, The Miz. The unlikely tandem secured the WWE Tag Team Championship on *SmackDown* territory following the unique talent exchange arrangement between *SmackDown* and *ECW* managing officials. The Shaman of Sexy's vanity reached new heights, much like his sports-entertainment career.

And Morrison has good reason to be confident. He has never been too far away from gold since his debut in 2005, capturing tag team gold as well as the Intercontinental Championship. The Shaman of Sexy was ultimately drafted to *ECW* during the 2007 Supplemental Draft on WWE.com, and his career was given new life. As the world can now see, Morrison has taken full advantage of his extreme home, and *ECW* may never be the same.

PROFILE:

THE MIZ®

HEIGHT
6-foot-1
WEIGHT
231 pounds
FROM
Cleveland, OH
SIGNATURE MOVE
The Mizard of Oz
WWE DEBUT
WWE Tag Team Champion
World Tag Team Champion

IF you ask self-proclaimed chick magnet The Miz, all the ladies want him and all the guys want to be him. And, quite frankly, it's hard to argue otherwise.

A devoted WWE fan his whole life, Mike 'The Miz' Mizanin competed on the fourth season of *'Tough Enough'* with hopes of winning a contract to become a WWE Superstar. After finishing as the runner-up, The Miz didn't give up on his dream and continued to train once the *'Tough Enough'* competition ended. Now, his hard work is being rewarded as the reality TV alum with the frat boy looks, over-confident humour and explosive intensity is living out his dream as a Superstar on *ECW*. Alongside John Morrison, The Miz won the WWE Tag Team Championship, defeating MVP and Matt Hardy on *SmackDown*. Since, the duo has dominated WWE's tag team division.

Undertaker

UMAGA

STONE COLD

Shelton BENJAMIN

JOHN CENA

MVP

MARK HENRY™

CARLITO
Caribbean Cool™

CHRIS JERICHO®

CM PUNK™

RANDY ORTON™

MR. KENNEDY™

PROFILE:

PAUL BURCHILL™

HEIGHT
6-foot-4
WEIGHT
247 pounds
FROM
Chelsea, England
SIGNATURE MOVE
Reverse Swinging Neckbreaker

PAUL BURCHILL is best described by his sister Katie Lea as the world's 'most beautiful, vicious man'. His 'beauty' may be debatable, but there's no denying 'The Ripper's' brutality and viciousness. This native Brit is hard-hitting in the ring and well-versed in the techniques of inflicting pain.

Making his debut in 2005 on *SmackDown*, Burchill originally aligned himself with fellow Brit, William Regal. The two had some success in the tag team division but in 2006 the pair parted ways. Later that year, Burchill was sidelined with an injury after taking a beating from Mark Henry. In January 2008, Paul Burchill returned to *Raw*, this time along with his sister, Katie Lea Burchill. The pair soon made an impact defeating Superstars like The Brian Kendrick and Mr Kennedy.

In late 2008, Burchill and his sister were drafted to *ECW* where the pair have continued to inflict pain on anyone who stands in their way. Only time will tell what the future holds for the Englishman known as 'The Ripper'.

GUESS THE ECW SUPERSTAR

Q1

I DESCRIBE MYSELF AS 'THE ALL-AMERICAN AMERICAN,' THE BEST OF THE BEST, AND THE HIGHEST OF THE HIGH. I FIRST GOT INTO AMATEUR WRESTLING WHEN I WAS JUST FIVE YEARS OLD. I DEFEATED MATT HARDY IN JANUARY 2008 FOR THE *ECW* CHAMPIONSHIP. I WAS BROUGHT TO *ECW* BY THEODORE LONG.

Q2

I MADE MY WWE DEBUT ON 26 MAY 2006. I AM A FORMER CRUISERWEIGHT CHAMPION AND THE LAST MAN TO HOLD THE CHAMPIONSHIP BEFORE THE TITLE WAS RETIRED. IT WAS BELIEVED THAT I WAS THE ILLEGITIMATE SON OF WWE OWNER, MR MCMAHON. YOU WILL OFTEN FIND ME HIDING UNDER THE RING.

Q3

I AM THE SMARTEST SUPERSTAR IN *ECW*. I AM A FORMER TEACHER WHO GOT FIRED FROM MY JOB WHEN SOME OF MY STUDENTS SAW ME PERFORMING ON *SMACKDOWN*. I WAS TRAINED BY WWE HALL OF FAMER, JOHNNY RODZ. I WEIGH 224 POUNDS AND I LIVE IN BAYSIDE, NEW YORK.

DJ GABRIEL ☐ CHRISTIAN ☐ HORNWOGGLE ☐

USING YOUR KNOWLEDGE OF THE *ECW* SUPERSTARS, CAN YOU MATCH EACH DESCRIPTION TO EACH SUPERSTAR?

Q4

I HAIL FROM THE UNITED KINGDOM, WHERE I SPENT MOST OF MY CAREER COMPETING IN EUROPE. IN NOVEMBER, I BROUGHT MY CHISELLED PHYSIQUE, WHICH I PRIDE MYSELF ON, TO THE LAND OF EXTREME. IN *ECW*, I OFFER PERSONAL LESSONS IN DANCING AND WRESTLING. I AM OFTEN SEEN ALONGSIDE ALICIA FOX.

Q5

I AM SMUG, EXTREMELY CONFIDENT AND BELIEVE MY VERY PRESENCE IS A GIFT TO SPORTS-ENTERTAINMENT FANS EVERYWHERE. TRUTH BE TOLD, I AM A NINE-TIME WORLD TAG TEAM CHAMPION AND THREE-TIME INTERCONTINENTAL CHAMPION, I EVEN WON A CHAMPIONSHIP IN MY VERY FIRST WWE MATCH.

Q6

I MADE MY *ECW* DEBUT IN 1993, MAKING ME THE LONGEST TENURED *ECW* ORIGINAL. MY BLUE COLLAR ETHIC IS SOMETHING THAT ALL ASPIRE TO, AND IT FINALLY PAID OFF WHEN I WON THE *ECW* WORLD CHAMPIONSHIP FROM TAZZ IN 2000. I AM THE FIRST SUPERSTAR EVER TO KICK OUT OF 'SUPERFLY' JIMMY SNUKA'S SUPERFLY SPLASH.

JACK SWAGGER ■ MATT STRIKER ■ TOMMY DREAMER ■

(ANSWERS: 1. JACK SWAGGER, 2. HORNSWOGGLE, 3. MATT STRIKER, 4. DJ GABRIEL, 5. CHRISTIAN, 6. TOMMY DREAMER)

ECW

EXTREME MAKEOVER

TOMMY DREAMER AND MATT HARDY ARE TWO OF THE MOST DEDICATED SUPERSTARS IN *ECW*. WHY NOT SHOW YOUR APPRECIATION FOR THEM BY COLOURING THE GUYS SOME NEW WRESTLING GEAR?

ECW SPOT THE DIFFERENCE

CHECK OUT THESE TWO SETS OF IMAGES. THEY LOOK THE SAME DON'T THEY? WELL THEY ARE NOT! OUR DESIGNERS HAVE MADE TEN TINY CHANGES TO EACH OF THEM. CAN YOU SPOT THEM ALL?

divas QUIZ

WE ALL KNOW THAT THE WWE DIVAS ARE THE HOTTEST WOMEN ON TELEVISION, BUT HOW MUCH MORE DO YOU KNOW ABOUT THESE SMOKIN' HOT WOMEN? LET'S FIND OUT!

Q1

WHO WAS THE FIRST HOLDER OF THE WWE DIVAS CHAMPIONSHIP?

- A: Michelle McCool ☐
- B: Mickie James ☐
- C: Jillian ☐

Q2

CAN YOU TELL WHICH DIVA THIS IS FROM JUST LOOKING AT HER EYES?

- A: Candice ☐
- B: Eve ☐
- C: Mickie James ☐

Q3

WHERE IS KELLY KELLY FROM?

- A: Jacksonville, FL ☐
- B: Memphis, TN ☐
- C: Austin, TX ☐

Q4

WHO WAS THE FIRST WWE WOMEN'S CHAMPION?

- A: Fabulous Moolah ☐
- B: Mae Young ☐
- C: Trish Stratus ☐

Q5

WHO IS BETH PHOENIX'S BOYFRIEND?

- A: CM Punk ☐
- B: Randy Orton ☐
- C: Santino Marella ☐

Q6

WHO IS THIS DIVA?

- A: Candice ☐
- B: Katie Lea Burchill ☐
- C: Melina ☐

Q7

WHICH OF THESE DIVAS IS FROM THE U.K?

- A: Alicia Fox ☐
- B: Tiffany ☐
- C: Katie Lea Burchill ☐

Q8

WHAT IS THIS DIVAS SIGNATURE MOVE?

- A: Widows Peak ☐
- B: Mick Kick ☐
- C: Hurricanrana ☐

Q9

WHO IS THIS DIVA?

- A: Brie Bella ☐
- B: Candice ☐
- C: Kelly Kelly ☐

Q10

WHO ONCE BROKE CANDICE'S JAW ON AN EPISODE OF *RAW*?

- A: Mickie James ☐
- B: Michelle McCool ☐
- C: Beth Phoenix ☐

(ANSWERS: 1.A, 2.C, 3.A, 4.A, 5.C, 6.C, 7.C, 8.B, 9.A, 10.C)

DESIGN

A DIVA

THE DIVAS ARE PUTTING ON THEIR ANNUAL FANCY DRESS CONTEST. HELP THEM OUT BY COLOURING IN THEIR COSTUMES!

PROFILE:

BIG SHOW®

HEIGHT
7-foot
WEIGHT
441 pounds
FROM
Tampa, FL
SIGNATURE MOVE
Chokeslam

REMINISCENT of Andre the Giant and Big John Studd before him, the pound-for-pound World's Largest Athlete is a feared competitor who can intimidate an opponent with his size and stare alone. Big Show's measurements are astounding: 441 pounds, 7-feet of raw girth and might, 22 EEEEE shoe size, 22 1/2 ring size and a 64-inch chest.

Big Show made his in-ring debut in WCW where he left a massive impression as The Giant, and captured the WCW Championship on two occasions, along with the WCW Tag Team Championships. The Giant had an immediate impact in WCW, focusing his attention on some of the biggest icons in the industry, from Hollywood Hulk Hogan to 'Nature Boy' Ric Flair.

In 1999, the mighty giant became a worldwide star upon signing with WWE. He continued to collide with Superstars of great renown and captured countless Championships, including the WWE Championship. From 'Stone Cold' Steve Austin to The Rock to Undertaker to Triple H, Big Show has battled and manhandled the top names in all of World Wrestling Entertainment.

After more than one year away from the ring, the immense monster re-emerged at *No Way Out 2008*, almost eight years to the date of his debut. Sporting a leaner physique and renewed appetite for destruction, Big Show returned to his dominant ways and continues to be a giant nightmare to anyone who steps in his path.

PROFILE:

EDGE®

HEIGHT
6-FOOT-5
WEIGHT
250 pounds
FROM
Toronto, Ontario
SIGNATURE MOVE
Spear
CAREER HIGHLIGHTS
WWE Champion
World Heavyweight Champion
World Tag Team Champion
WWE Tag Team Champion
Intercontinental Champion
WCW United States Champion

EDGE made his WWE debut in 1998 after years of training and hard work on the independent scene. He was trained by some of the best in the business, including Bret Hart and his father, the legendary Stu Hart. With such great experience behind him, it was no surprise when Edge showed up in WWE and made an immediate impact. In July 1999, Edge won his first major championship, the Intercontinental Championship from Jeff Jarrett.

Soon Edge was joined by his 'Brother', Christian and the pair would take the tag team division by storm, capturing the WWE Tag Team Championship on seven different occasions. Their battles with the Hardys transformed the tag team division and produced some of the best matches in the history of WWE.

The pair split in 2001 and Edge found his niche working as a singles competitor. In 2001, Edge won the *King Of The Ring* Tournament and would go on to capture the Intercontinental Championship for a second time.

Since then, Edge has gone from strength to strength, capturing both the WWE and World Heavyweight Championship on several occasions, hitting his stride as a consistent main event performer, and never shying away from controversy. Known as both the Rated-R Superstar and the Ultimate Opportunist, Edge will go to any means possible to walk out of the arena with gold around his waist. He has cashed in Money in the Bank contracts to win the Championship against a battered opponent on two separate occasions, and has sought preferential treatment by entering into a romance with *SmackDown* General Manager Vickie Guerrero. Still, whether you love Edge or hate him, you cannot deny the impact he has had in his decade of decadence and can only guess what his next move will be.

WORD SEARCH

CAN YOU SPOT ALL TEN OF THE *SMACKDOWN* SUPERSTARS HIDING IN THIS WORD SEARCH? REMEMBER, THE WORDS CAN GO FORWARDS, BACKWARDS AND EVEN DIAGONALLY!

E	W	E	I	U	C	N	S	B	K	V	B	H	U	P
M	D	L	U	U	K	A	X	Y	F	M	T	V	V	P
H	U	G	H	H	N	M	U	J	W	U	H	B	X	J
I	X	O	E	Q	U	D	T	V	R	X	D	O	V	E
V	R	H	L	A	E	L	E	T	B	H	U	W	D	F
R	A	J	P	N	C	O	R	R	Z	T	S	T	P	F
L	H	L	I	S	Y	G	W	L	T	C	T	B	T	H
N	Q	A	R	F	I	Y	Y	O	G	A	M	B	G	A
Z	K	U	T	U	R	T	V	Q	H	J	K	X	L	R
U	M	A	G	A	W	T	L	J	H	S	D	E	P	D
I	C	S	E	B	C	O	L	Z	W	C	G	N	R	Y
T	U	R	T	H	O	C	S	D	E	J	D	I	G	Q
O	B	O	V	V	V	S	K	A	L	T	M	I	B	A
V	I	C	K	I	E	G	U	E	R	R	E	R	O	Q
R	Y	K	R	Y	D	E	N	N	E	K	R	M	U	A

- BIG SHOW
- EDGE
- JEFF HARDY
- MR KENNEDY
- R TRUTH
- SCOTTY GOLDMAN
- TRIPLE H
- UMAGA
- UNDERTAKER
- VICKIE GUERRERO

CROSSWORD

USE ALL YOUR HIGHLY DEVELOPED SKILLS AND CUNNING TO SOLVE THE CLUES AND REVEAL THE ANSWERS!

ACROSS

5. A phenominal undefeated streak at *WrestleMania*
8. The gold standard!
9. The more clever cousin
10. From the island of Samoa

DOWN

1. *SmackDown's* General Manager
2. This guy makes a mean BBQ sauce!
3. His brother is named Primo
4. A former *SmackDown* commentator
6. Won the WWE Championship at *Armageddon 2008*
7. The World's largest athlete

PROFILE:

MVP™

HEIGHT
6-foot-3
WEIGHT
249 pounds
FROM
Miami, FL
SIGNATURE MOVE
The Playmaker

MONTEL VONTAVIOUS PORTER made his WWE debut in 2006 after then General Manager, Theodore Long, tempted the free agent with a lucrative contract agreement. MVP soon proved he was worth his asking price by capturing the United States Championship after a brutal Best Two-Out-of-Three Falls Match. MVP held the Championship for over a year, making him one of the longest reigning champions in history.

MVP soon found himself WWE Tag Team Champions with Matt Hardy, the No. 1 contender to his United States Championship. Although the pair were not the best of friends, they made very effective champions, even though MVP constantly insisted that he was the entire reason for their success. Unfortunately for Matt, MVP's true motive for partnering with him was to keep him from challenging him in singles competition. When Matt pushed the issue, MVP double-crossed him and caused Matt a serious injury, forcing him to leave *SmackDown* once again. Upon his return, Hardy not only cost MVP the Money in the Bank Ladder match at *WrestleMania XXIV*, but inevitability the United States Championship as well.

R-TRUTH™

HEIGHT
6-FOOT-2
WEIGHT
228 pounds
FROM
Charlotte, NC
SIGNATURE MOVE
The Consequence

SMACK DOWN

R-TRUTH knows all about hard times. Growing up in the rough neighbourhoods of Charlotte, NC, he admits he made some bad decisions in the past. But, R-Truth believes those choices have made him into a much more formidable opponent in the ring. As a two-time former WWE Hardcore Champion, R-Truth is as tough as he is talented.

For Truth, his talent is a blessing. He believes he has been given a second chance in life and has no intention of wasting it. After spending some time in prison, Truth realised that a change was needed from within to get away from a life of crime - a change that has brought him to WWE and a much more positive life. Truth wanted to keep far away from the path he took growing up and WWE turned out to be his light at the end of the tunnel.

Truth calls WWE 'a new struggle, but a welcome struggle.' He has spent years working on his craft and is ready to open the eyes of the WWE Universe to 'the Truth.'

QUIZ

DO YOU KNOW EVERYTHING THERE IS TO KNOW ABOUT WWE *SMACKDOWN* AND ITS SUPERSTARS? LET'S FIND OUT!

Q1

WHAT COLOUR ARE THE *SMACKDOWN* RING ROPES?

A: Blue ☐
B: Red ☐
C: Black ☐

Q2

WHO IS THIS *SMACKDOWN* STAR?

A: Jamie Noble ☐
B: Undertaker ☐
C: Kung Fu Naki ☐

Q3

WHERE IS RYAN BRADDOCK FROM?

A: Chicago
B: New York
C: Memphis

Q4

WHO IS THIS *SMACKDOWN* ANNOUNCER?

A: Michael Cole
B: Jim Ross
C: Tazz

Q5

IN WHAT YEAR WAS *SMACKDOWN* FIRST BROADCAST?

A: 1998
B: 1999
C: 2000

Q6

WHO WAS THE FIRST GENERAL MANAGER OF *SMACKDOWN*?

A: Stephanie McMahon
B: Theodore Long
C: Vickie Guerrero

Q7

IN WHAT YEAR DID MARIA MAKE HER WWE DEBUT?

A: 2003
B: 2004
C: 2005

Q8

WHO IS THIS *SMACKDOWN* DIVA?

A: Maryse
B: Michelle McCool
C: Nikki Bella

Q9

WHICH OF THESE SUPERSTARS HAS BEEN ON THE *SMACKDOWN* ROSTER THE LONGEST?

A: Edge
B: Undertaker
C: Carlito

Q10

IN WHAT YEAR DID EZEKIEL JACKSON MAKE HIS WWE DEBUT?

A: 2007
B: 2008
C: 2009

(ANSWERS: 1.A, 2.C, 3.A, 4.B, 5.B, 6.A, 7.B, 8.A, 9.B, 10.B)

PROFILE:

THE BRIAN KENDRICK®

HEIGHT
5-foot-8
WEIGHT
184 pounds
FROM
Venice, CA
SIGNATURE MOVE
Sliced Bread No. 2

SMACK DOWN®

THE BRIAN KENDRICK is one of the most unusual and arrogant Superstars on *SmackDown*. Originally, he was trained by Shawn Michaels at his academy in Texas. Being one of the smallest trainees in his class, Kendrick soon realised that to get noticed in the sport, he would have to hone his skills and collect styles from all over the world.

Kendrick made his way to Japan, where he developed his high-flying and hard hitting repertoire of moves. When he returned to the States, he worked on the independent scene before making his WWE debut in 2003. Kendrick's original tenure was short lived as he stayed with the company for little over a year before returning to the independent circuit to further develop his skills.

Two years later, in 2005, Kendrick returned to WWE and set the tag team division on fire with his then partner, Paul London. The pair captured the WWE Tag Team Championship twice before splitting in 2008.

The Brian Kendrick was the first Superstar to switch brands in successive years as a result of the WWE Supplemental Draft. His determination is quickly distinguishing him from WWE's other high-flying Superstars. And with his associate, Ezekiel Jackson, in his corner, he promises to make a tremendous impact on *SmackDown*.

PROFILE:

MR KENNEDY®

HEIGHT
6-FOOT-2
WEIGHT
235 pounds
FROM
Green Bay, WI
SIGNATURE MOVE
Mic Check

SMACK DOWN

MR KENNEDY is one of the hungriest Superstars in the whole WWE. Since his debut in 2005, the arrogant, yet strangely likeable Wisconsin native has made a huge impact on the WWE Universe. He won the Money in The Bank Ladder Match at *WrestleMania* 23 and could have gone on to win the WWE Championship had it not been for a serious injury.

So what fuels Mr Kennedy's desire? Maybe it is his huge ego; maybe it's greed. Maybe it's his memories of growing up in the frozen tundra of Green Bay, watching legends such as Hulk Hogan, Randy 'Macho Man' Savage and later, 'Stone Cold' Steve Austin. His toughness was forged by a stint in the U.S. Army and battling before hundreds - not thousands, hundreds - of onlookers in dirty rings while on the independent wrestling circuit before hitting the big time in WWE. If nothing else, Mr Kennedy is a survivor who is living his dream.

Now, back on *SmackDown*, you can bet that Kennedy will have his sights firmly set on the one prize that has so narrowly eluded him thus far, the WWE Championship.

GUESS THE SUPERSTAR

SMACK DOWN

Q1

I AM THE DEFINITION OF RINGSIDE INTIMIDATION. BORN IN GUYANA, I MOVED TO HARLEM WHERE THE ROUGH STREETS HELPED RAISE ME. I ENTERED WWE AS AN ASSOCIATE OF THE BRIAN KENDRICK AND SERVED AS HIS BODYGUARD. I MADE MY DEBUT IN 2008.

Q2

I AM FROM LONG ISLAND, NEW YORK. I MADE MY WWE DEBUT ALONG SIDE MY BROTHER ZACK IN 2007. I WEIGH 221 POUNDS. AT *ARMAGEDDON 2007* I HELPED EDGE RETAIN THE WORLD HEAVYWEIGHT CHAMPIONSHIP AND I AM NOW PROUD TO CALL MYSELF A MEMBER OF THE FAMILY!

Q3

I AM A FORMER CRUISERWEIGHT CHAMPION, AND WAS ONE OF THE LONGEST-REIGNING CHAMPIONS IN WWE HISTORY. I CAPTURED THE CHAMPIONSHIP AT THE 2006 EDITION OF THE *ROYAL RUMBLE*. PRIOR TO ENTERING WWE, I WAS A STAR IN WCW, WHERE I HELD THE CRUISERWEIGHT AND HARDCORE CHAMPIONSHIPS.

SHELTON BENJAMIN ■

EZEKIEL JACKSON ■

CURT HAWKINS ■

SO YOU KNOW IT ALL DO YA? WELL LET'S SEE JUST HOW MUCH YOU KNOW ABOUT THE TOUGH AS NAILS SUPERSTARS OF *SMACKDOWN*. MATCH EACH DESCRIPTION TO THE CORRECT SUPERSTAR AND WHO KNOWS; MAYBE YOU WILL PROVE THAT YOU HAVE WHAT IT TAKES TO BE PART OF WORLD WRESTLING ENTERTAINMENT.

Q4

I AM PERHAPS THE MOST GIFTED ATHLETE IN WWE TODAY. I GREW UP ON THE MEAN STREETS OF ORANGEBURG, SOUTH CAROLINA. I AM AN EXPERT VIDEO GAMES PLAYER AND EVEN WON THE ANNUAL *WRESTLEMANIA* FAN FEST CHAMPIONSHIP TOURNAMENT THREE YEARS IN A ROW.

Q5

I AM A HULKING 6-FOOT-8, 300-POUNDER. I AM TRAINED IN SEVERAL DIFFERENT FIGHTING STYLES, INCLUDING SAMBO, JUDO AND KICKBOXING. I AM A FORMER U.S. OPEN HEAVYWEIGHT SAMBO CHAMPION AND U.S. KICKBOXING ASSOCIATION INTERNATIONAL GRAPPLING CHAMPION.

Q6

HAILING FROM SAN JUAN, I AM THE YOUNGER BROTHER OF FORMER INTERCONTINENTAL AND U.S. CHAMPION CARLITO AND THE SON OF LEGENDARY PUERTO RICO WRESTLER CARLOS COLON. AT THE TENDER AGE OF JUST 17, I MADE MY IN-RING DEBUT AFTER LEARNING THE ROPES FROM MY DAD.

PRIMO ▢ HURRICANE HELMS ▢ VLADIMIR KOZLOV ▢

(ANSWERS: 1. EZEKIEL JACKSON, 2. CURT HAWKINS, 3. HURRICANE HELMS, 4. SHELTON BENJAMIN, 5. VLADIMIR KOZLOV, 6. PRIMO)

ANAGRAMS

Q1 GOGLE SHWORN

Q2 HELICAL COME

Q3 LILAC PUB HURL

Q4 CRAM HMM ON

Q5 CRAG JAW KEGS

ONCE AGAIN, OUR EDITOR HERE AT PEDIGREE PICKED AN ARGUMENT WITH THE ICON OF EXTREME, TOMMY DREAMER AND CAUGHT HIMSELF A FEW SHOTS WITH A KENDO STICK. NOW HE HAS GOT ALL THE SUPERSTARS AND CHAMPIONSHIPS MIXED UP! DO US A FAVOUR AND REARRANGE THE LETTERS SO THEY MAKE SENSE!

Q6 AN CHE NOJ

Q7 PROD DRIPEY

Q8 A DIVANS CHIP MOPISH

Q9 ALI LANGI CRIA

Q10 BOTH HE EX NIP

(ANSWERS: 1. HORNSWOGGLE, 2. MICHAEL COLE, 3. PAUL BURCHILL, 4. MR McMAHON, 5. JACK SWAGGER, 6. JOHN CENA, 7. RODDY PIPER, 8. DIVAS CHAMPIONSHIP, 9. LILIAN GARCIA, 10. BETH PHOENIX)

PAY-PER-VIEW QUIZ

THE WWE PUTS ON SO MANY GREAT SHOWS EACH AND EVERY MONTH OF THE YEAR. HOW MUCH DO YOU KNOW ABOUT THESE INCREDIBLE EVENTS?

Q1

IN WHAT YEAR DID THE FIRST *ROYAL RUMBLE* TAKE PLACE?

A: 1998 ☐
B: 1988 ☐
C: 1989 ☐

Q2

WHO IS THIS SUPERSTAR THAT WON THE FIRST-EVER *ROYAL RUMBLE*?

A: Hacksaw Jim Duggan ☐
B: Hulk Hogan ☐
C: Sgt. Slaughter ☐

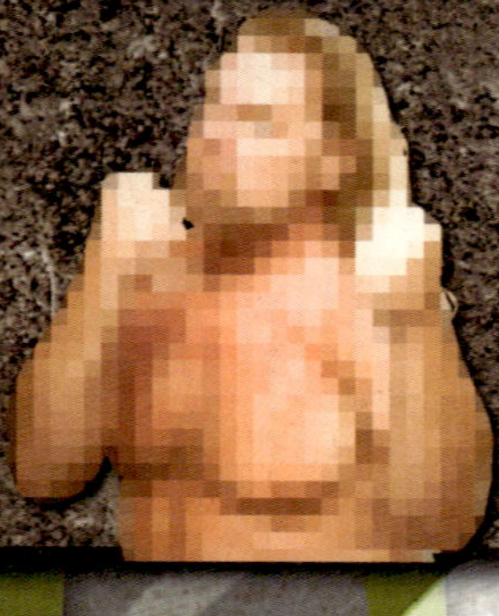

Q3

IN WHICH STATE DID *VENGEANCE: NIGHT OF CHAMPIONS 2007* HAIL FROM?

A: Texas ☐
B: California ☐
C: New York ☐

Q4

WHO DID TRIPLE H FACE AT *UNFORGIVEN 2004*?

A: Umaga ☐
B: Shawn Michaels ☐
C: Randy Orton ☐

Q5

FOR WHICH PAY-PER-VIEW IS THIS LOGO FROM?

A: *Vengeance* ☐
B: *No Way Out* ☐
C: *WrestleMania* ☐

Q6

WHO WAS THE FIRST MAN TO WIN A MATCH AT *WRESTLEMANIA*?

A: Tito Santana ☐
B: King Kong Bundy ☐
C: Ultimate Warrior ☐

Q7

IN WHAT YEAR DID *WRESTLEMANIA* CELEBRATE ITS TWENTIETH ANNIVERSARY?

A: 2003 ☐
B: 2004 ☐
C: 2005 ☐

Q8

WHO WAS THE SPECIAL REFEREE IN THE MAIN EVENT AT *CYBER SUNDAY 2007*?

A: Mick Foley ☐
B: Stone Cold Steve Austin ☐
C: Roddy Piper ☐

Q9

IN WHAT YEAR DID WWE FIRST INTRODUCE THE *ONE NIGHT STAND* PAY-PER-VIEW?

A: 2004 ☐
B: 2005 ☐
C: 2006 ☐

Q10

HOW MANY TIMES HAS UNDERTAKER COMPETED AGAINST KANE AT *WRESTLEMANIA*?

A: Zero ☐
B: Once ☐
C: Twice ☐

(ANSWERS: 1.B, 2.A, 3.A, 4.C, 5.C, 6.A, 7.B, 8.B, 9.B, 10.C)

CHAMPIONS QUIZ

TO GET TO THE TOP OF WWE, YOU HAVE TO DEFEAT SOME OF THE GREATEST ATHLETES IN THE WORLD. IN THIS QUIZ, WE TAKE A LOOK AT THE CHAMPIONS OF WWE AND THEIR RISE TO THE TOP!

Q1

WHO DID JOHN CENA DEFEAT FOR HIS FIRST WWE CHAMPIONSHIP?

- A: JBL ☐
- B: Chris Jericho ☐
- C: Batista ☐

Q2

WHO IS THIS WWE SUPERSTAR?

- A: Triple H ☐
- B: Chris Jericho ☐
- C: Jeff Hardy ☐

Q3

IN WHAT YEAR WAS THE WORLD HEAVYWEIGHT CHAMPIONSHIP INTRODUCED TO WWE?

A: 2001 ☐
B: 2002 ☐
C: 2003 ☐

Q4

WHO WAS THE FIRST HOLDER OF THE WORLD HEAVYWEIGHT CHAMPIONSHIP IN WWE?

A: Randy Orton ☐
B: Eddie Guerrero ☐
C: Triple H ☐

Q5

WHO DID JOHN MORRISON DEFEAT FOR HIS FIRST *ECW* CHAMPIONSHIP?

A: CM Punk ☐
B: Matt Hardy ☐
C: Mark Henry ☐

Q6

HOW MANY TIMES HAS SHAWN MICHAELS HELD THE INTERCONTINENTAL CHAMPIONSHIP?

A: Once ☐
B: Twice ☐
C: Three times ☐

Q7

WHICH CHAMPIONSHIP BELT IS THIS?

A: World Heavyweight ☐
B: WWE ☐
C: Divas ☐

Q8

WHO DID CARLITO DEFEAT TO EARN HIS FIRST UNITED STATES CHAMPIONSHIP?

A: John Cena ☐
B: Edge ☐
C: Primo ☐

Q9

WHO DEFEATED MATT HARDY FOR THE UNITED STATES CHAMPIONSHIP IN 2008?

A: MVP ☐
B: Shelton Benjamin ☐
C: Finlay ☐

Q10

IN WHAT YEAR WAS THE WWE WOMEN'S CHAMPIONSHIP FIRST INTRODUCED?

A: 1990 ☐
B: 1956 ☐
C: 1969 ☐

(ANSWERS: 1.A, 2.C, 3.B, 4.C, 5.A, 6.C, 7.B, 8.A, 9.B, 10.B)

ANSWERS

PAGE 8

Q	R	G	E	A	W	R	S	D	O	U	H	L	L	R
V	N	C	N	V	W	E	Z	F	C	M	I	C	E	O
J	R	G	A	J	B	L	T	R	M	Y	V	M	W	N
H	H	U	K	E	X	G	C	R	Y	S	U	S	O	S
Q	S	P	D	V	B	G	H	W	O	Q	A	L	P	I
R	L	A	V	M	H	I	Z	J	I	A	Y	G	O	M
P	H	M	X	V	G	Z	O	M	H	I	M	S	Z	M
S	A	N	M	I	C	H	A	E	L	C	O	L	E	O
I	D	L	T	Z	N	P	I	O	R	X	S	E	T	N
H	B	V	Y	C	X	L	E	C	I	D	N	A	C	S
O	F	W	E	A	R	O	T	F	Q	N	E	B	C	M
R	U	N	N	A	L	D	P	F	W	O	Y	B	T	X
E	A	B	H	F	H	T	B	A	P	B	R	T	A	F
C	A	C	V	J	L	V	Z	F	D	G	L	V	Q	G
J	O	I	X	R	J	V	Q	Y	M	A	N	U	K	K

PAGE 30

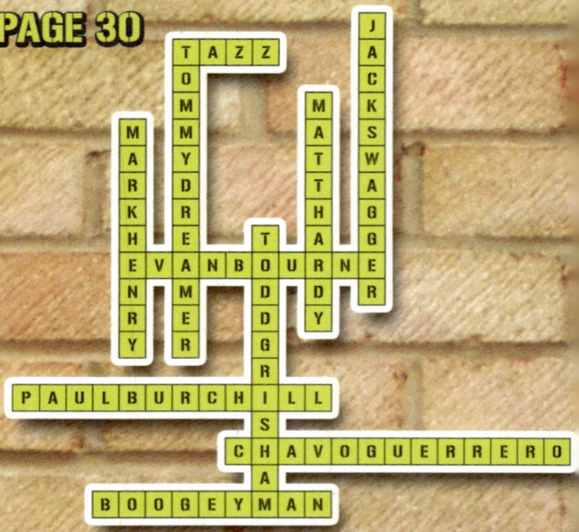

PAGE 9

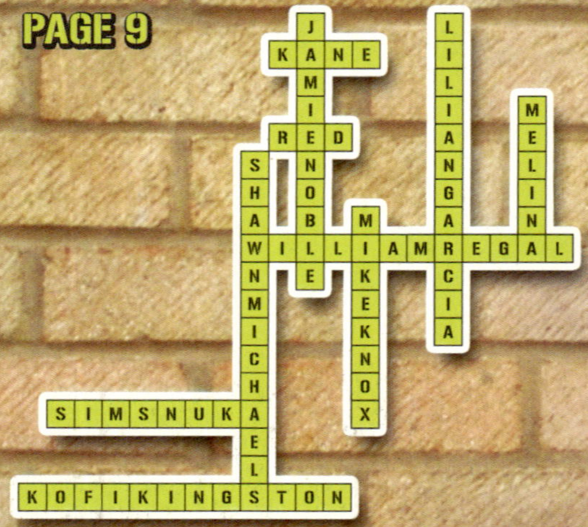

PAGE 31

R	A	Y	G	X	Y	O	O	U	A	W	T	Y	B	X
I	I	T	D	A	F	O	J	L	V	E	O	N	N	E
A	P	C	L	R	C	X	I	V	L	I	N	A	W	D
V	P	N	K	M	A	C	F	G	Y	N	Y	F	F	S
M	I	Y	D	Y	I	H	G	V	A	Y	A	F	M	Y
F	M	P	O	A	O	O	T	N	K	C	T	I	P	I
P	U	V	F	U	W	R	Y	T	Y	E	L	T	O	K
J	U	O	N	S	M	L	T	Z	A	W	A	R	K	Q
M	X	K	N	T	H	E	M	I	Z	M	S	X	L	P
Z	R	R	Q	R	C	R	B	O	Z	E	E	G	X	M
M	O	L	E	I	R	B	A	G	J	D	Z	T	X	P
H	Y	L	M	D	P	T	Y	V	O	H	N	U	V	D
D	U	S	T	Y	R	H	O	D	E	S	A	L	T	U
C	N	U	D	Y	H	S	C	D	Z	F	A	M	V	K
T	Q	S	Y	Q	M	T	F	B	C	Q	P	X	R	M

PAGE 42

PAGE 52

E	W	E	I	U	C	N	S	B	K	V	B	H	U	P
M	D	L	U	U	K	A	X	Y	F	M	T	V	V	P
H	U	G	H	H	N	M	U	J	W	U	H	B	X	J
I	X	O	E	Q	U	D	T	V	R	X	D	O	V	E
V	R	H	L	A	E	L	E	T	B	H	U	W	D	F
R	A	J	P	N	C	O	R	R	Z	T	S	T	P	F
L	H	L	I	S	Y	G	W	L	T	C	T	B	T	H
N	Q	A	R	F	I	Y	Y	O	G	A	M	B	G	A
Z	K	U	T	U	R	T	V	Q	H	J	K	X	L	R
U	M	A	G	A	W	T	L	J	H	S	D	E	P	D
I	C	S	E	B	C	O	L	Z	W	C	G	N	R	Y
T	U	R	T	H	O	C	S	D	E	J	D	I	G	Q
O	B	O	V	V	V	S	K	A	L	T	M	I	B	A
V	I	C	K	I	E	G	U	E	R	R	E	R	O	Q
R	Y	K	R	Y	D	E	N	N	E	K	R	M	U	A

PAGE 43

PAGE 53